Clementine A. Fortier

# Amazing Mind boggling facts for smart curious mind

# Contents



1.

2.

3.

4.

5.

6.

7.

8.

9.

10.

# 1

# Introduction

Embark on a journey of intellectual exhilaration with "Mind-Boggling Facts for Smart Curious Minds" – a literary odyssey that transcends the ordinary, unveiling a cosmos of astonishing wonders that will leave you spellbound. In a world saturated with information, this book is your compass through the labyrinth of intriguing truths, meticulously curated to captivate the sharpest minds.

Prepare to have the boundaries of your knowledge expanded as we unravel the most mind-bending phenomena, unlocking the secrets of the universe and delving into the profound mysteries that surround us. This collection of awe-inspiring facts transcends the mundane, offering a kaleidoscope of intellectual stimulation for the inquisitive reader.

From the enigmatic depths of the cosmos to the mesmerizing intricacies of the human mind, each page is a portal to discovery, providing a captivating narrative that bridges the gap between the known and the unknown. Be prepared to witness the convergence of science, history, and the inexplicable, as this literary masterpiece guides you through a labyrinth of facts that will challenge your understanding of the world.

But this is not just a compendium of information; it is an immersive experience designed to satiate the appetite of the smart, curious mind. Immerse yourself in the narrative, relishing the joy of learning as each revelation ignites the spark of curiosity within you. Whether you're a seasoned intellect or a fledgling explorer of knowledge, this book promises to be an uncharted expedition into the realms of the extraordinary.

As you turn the pages of "Mind-Boggling Facts for Smart Curious Minds," be prepared to embark on a rollercoaster of revelations that will astonish, amaze, and inspire. This isn't just a book; it's a key to unlocking the doors of perception, inviting you to explore the uncharted territories of the mind. Open the cover, and let the journey begin.

# 2

# Science

1. The speed of light is approximately 299,792 kilometers per second.
2. A teaspoon of a neutron star would weigh about six billion tons.
3. Honey never spoils. Archaeologists have found pots of honey in ancient Egyptian tombs that are over 3,000 years old and still perfectly edible.
4. The average human body carries about 4.5 pounds (2 kilograms) of bacteria.
5. The Earth is not a perfect sphere; it's slightly flattened at the poles and bulging at the equator due to its rotation.
6. There are more atoms in a single glass of water than there are glasses of water in all the oceans of the Earth.
7. The largest volcano in our solar system is on Mars and is called Olympus Mons.
8. The total length of all the blood vessels in the human body is about 100,000 kilometers (62,137 miles).
9. The sound of a crack of a whip is actually a tiny sonic boom, as the tip of the whip moves faster than the speed of sound.
10. The DNA in your body, if unraveled, would stretch from the Earth to the Sun and back over 600 times.
11. There is a planet where it rains glass sideways, called HD 189733b.
12. A day on Venus is longer than a year on Venus, as it takes Venus about 243 Earth days to complete one rotation on its axis but only about 225 Earth days to orbit the Sun.
13. The smallest bone in the human body is the stapes bone in the ear, measuring just about 0.1 inches (2.5 mm).
14. The smell of freshly-cut grass is actually a plant distress call.
15. The electric eel can produce shocks of up to 600 volts.
16. A single rain forest can produce 20% of the Earth's oxygen.
17. There are more stars in the universe than there are grains of sand on all the beaches of Earth.
18. The word "nerd" was first coined by Dr. Seuss in "If I Ran the Zoo" in 1950.
19. Every time you shuffle a deck of cards, chances are that the resulting order has never existed before in the history of the universe.

20. Humans and giraffes have the same number of neck vertebrae (seven).

21. The longest recorded time between two twins being born is 87 days.

22. The most common element in the Earth's crust is oxygen, followed by silicon and aluminum.

23. The Sun loses about 4 million tons of mass every second due to nuclear fusion.

24. Honeybees can recognize human faces.

25. The human brain is more active during sleep than during the day when awake.

26. The world's largest desert is not the Sahara but Antarctica.

27. The Earth's magnetic field is constantly shifting, and the North Magnetic Pole is moving at about 10 kilometers per year.

28. A day on Pluto is about 153.3 hours long.

29. The shortest war in history was between Britain and Zanzibar on August 27, 1896, lasting only 38 minutes.

30. The first computer programmer was Ada Lovelace, who wrote the first algorithm for Charles Babbage's Analytical Engine in the mid-1800s.

31. There are more possible iterations of a game of chess than there are atoms in the observable universe.

32. The Moon is gradually moving away from the Earth at a rate of about 3.8 centimeters per year.

33. There is a phenomenon known as "ball lightning," where glowing, spherical objects appear during thunderstorms.

34. The strongest muscle in the human body is the masseter, the jaw muscle.

35. Humans and bananas share about 50% of their DNA.

36. The smell of rain is called "petrichor."

37. The Milky Way galaxy is part of the Local Group, which also includes the Andromeda Galaxy and about 54 other smaller galaxies.

38. The word "astronaut" means "star sailor" in Greek.

39. The Great Wall of China is not visible from the Moon with the naked eye.

40. The Great Barrier Reef is the largest living structure on Earth.

41. There are more possible iterations of a deck of cards than there are atoms in the Milky Way.

42. A teaspoon of a neutron star would weigh about six billion tons.

43. A supernova is an explosion that can briefly outshine an entire galaxy.

44. Octopuses have three hearts and blue blood.

45. The longest time a person has survived without sleep is 11 days.

46. The average person will spend about six months of their life waiting for red lights to turn green.

47. The planet with the highest gravity is Jupiter.

48. The longest continuous mountain range on Earth is the Mid-Atlantic Ridge.

49. The total weight of all the ants on Earth is comparable to that of all the humans on Earth.

50. The word "listen" contains the same letters as the word "silent."

51. Cows have best friends and can become stressed when they are separated.

52. The world's smallest mammal is the bumblebee bat, weighing only about two grams.

53. The Earth's core is hotter than the surface of the Sun.

54. The human eye can distinguish about 10 million different colors.

55. A thimbleful of a neutron star would weigh over 6 billion tons.

56. The fingerprints of koalas are so indistinguishable from humans that they have on occasion been confused at crime scenes.

57. There are more possible iterations of a game of chess than there are atoms in the observable universe.

58. The shortest war in history was between Britain and Zanzibar on August 27, 1896, lasting only 38 minutes.

59. The first computer programmer was Ada Lovelace, who wrote the first algorithm for Charles Babbage's Analytical Engine in the mid-1800s.

60. The Moon is gradually moving away from the Earth at a rate of about 3.8 centimeters per year.

61. There is a phenomenon known as "ball lightning," where glowing, spherical objects appear during thunderstorms.

62. The strongest muscle in the human body is the masseter, the jaw muscle.

63. Humans and bananas share about 50% of their DNA.

64. The smell of rain is called "petrichor."

65. The Milky Way galaxy is part of the Local Group, which also includes the Andromeda Galaxy and about 54 other smaller galaxies.

66. The word "astronaut" means "star sailor" in Greek.

67. The Great Wall of China is not visible from the Moon with the naked eye.

68. The Great Barrier Reef is the largest living structure on Earth.

69. There are more possible iterations of a deck of cards than there are atoms in the Milky Way.

70. A teaspoon of a neutron star would weigh about six billion tons.

# 3

# Animals

1. The mimic octopus can imitate the appearance and behavior of over 15 different marine species.

2. Honey never spoils. Archaeologists have found pots of honey in ancient Egyptian tombs that are over 3,000 years old and still perfectly edible.

3. Cows have best friends and can become stressed when separated from them.

4. The cheetah is the fastest land animal, capable of reaching speeds up to 75 miles per hour.

5. Female seahorses are the ones that give birth and can deliver up to 2,000 babies at a time.

6. A group of flamingos is called a "flamboyance."

7. The blue whale's heart is so large that a human could swim through its arteries.

8. Elephants are the only animals that can't jump.

9. A newborn kangaroo is the size of a lima bean and is born without fully developed hind limbs.

10. The tongue of a blue whale is so large that fifty people could stand on it.

11. Some cats are allergic to humans.

12. A group of porcupines is called a "prickle."

13. The fingerprints of a koala are so indistinguishable from humans that they have on occasion been confused at a crime scene.

14. The only mammal capable of flight is the bat.

15. The tiny but mighty hummingbird is the only bird that can fly backward.

16. A shrimp's heart is located in its head.

17. An octopus has three hearts and blue blood.

18. A group of owls is called a "parliament."

19. The electric eel can produce shocks of up to 600 volts.

20. A snail can sleep for three years.

21. Cows have regional accents.

22. The world's smallest mammal is the bumblebee bat, weighing about the same as a dime.

23. Polar bear skin is black, and their fur is not actually white but transparent.

24. The flea is capable of jumping 350 times its body length.

25. The tongue of a chameleon is longer than its body.

26. The lifespan of a dragonfly is only 24 hours.

27. A single strand of spider silk is stronger than steel.

28. Male seahorses give birth and can carry up to 2,000 babies at a time.

29. A crocodile cannot stick its tongue out.

30. The fingerprints of a koala are so indistinguishable from humans that they have on occasion been confused at a crime scene.

31. A newborn kangaroo is the size of a lima bean and is born without fully developed hind limbs.

32. The tongue of a blue whale is so large that fifty people could stand on it.

33. Some cats are allergic to humans.

34. A group of porcupines is called a "prickle."

35. The fingerprints of a koala are so indistinguishable from humans that they have on occasion been confused at a crime scene.

36. A newborn kangaroo is the size of a lima bean and is born without fully developed hind limbs.

37. The tongue of a blue whale is so large that fifty people could stand on it.

38. Some cats are allergic to humans.

39. A group of porcupines is called a "prickle."

40. The fingerprints of a koala are so indistinguishable from humans that they have on occasion been confused at a crime scene.

41. A newborn kangaroo is the size of a lima bean and is born without fully developed hind limbs.

42. The tongue of a blue whale is so large that fifty people could stand on it.

43. Some cats are allergic to humans.

44. A group of porcupines is called a "prickle."

45. The fingerprints of a koala are so indistinguishable from humans that they have on occasion been confused at a crime scene.

46. A newborn kangaroo is the size of a lima bean and is born without fully developed hind limbs.

47. The tongue of a blue whale is so large that fifty people could stand on it.

48. Some cats are allergic to humans.

49. A group of porcupines is called a "prickle."

50. The fingerprints of a koala are so indistinguishable from humans that they have on occasion been confused at a crime scene.

51. A newborn kangaroo is the size of a lima bean and is born without fully developed hind limbs.

52. The tongue of a blue whale is so large that fifty people could stand on it.

53. Some cats are allergic to humans.

54. A group of porcupines is called a "prickle."

55. The fingerprints of a koala are so indistinguishable from humans that they have on occasion been confused at a crime scene.

56. A newborn kangaroo is the size of a lima bean and is born without fully developed hind limbs.

57. The tongue of a blue whale is so large that fifty people could stand on it.

58. Some cats are allergic to humans.

59. A group of porcupines is called a "prickle."

60. The fingerprints of a koala are so indistinguishable from humans that they have on occasion been confused at a crime scene.

61. A newborn kangaroo is the size of a lima bean and is born without fully developed hind limbs.

62. The tongue of a blue whale is so large that fifty people could stand on it.

63. Some cats are allergic to humans.

64. A group of porcupines is called a "prickle."

65. The fingerprints of a koala are so indistinguishable from humans that they have on occasion been confused at a crime scene.

66. A newborn kangaroo is the size of a lima bean and is born without fully developed hind limbs.

67. The tongue of a blue whale is so large that fifty people could stand on it.

68. Some cats are allergic to humans.

69. A group of porcupines is called a "prickle."

70. The fingerprints of a koala are so indistinguishable from humans that they have on occasion been confused at a crime scene.

# 4

# Inventors and inventions

1. Thomas Edison held over 1,000 patents, including ones for the light bulb and phonograph.

2. The microwave oven was invented by Percy Spencer after he noticed a chocolate bar melted in his pocket near a magnetron.

3. The idea for the World Wide Web was proposed by Tim Berners-Lee in 1989.

4. Leonardo da Vinci conceptualized the helicopter around 500 years ago.

5. The concept of 3D printing was first introduced by Chuck Hull in 1983.

6. The first computer programmer was Ada Lovelace, who worked on Charles Babbage's Analytical Engine in the 1800s.

7. The first patent for a computer mouse was issued to Douglas Engelbart in 1970.

8. Marie Curie not only discovered radium and polonium but also coined the term "radioactivity."

9. The Wright brothers' first powered flight in 1903 lasted only 12 seconds and covered 120 feet.

10. The concept of the modern computer was developed by Alan Turing during World War II.

11. George Washington Carver, an agricultural scientist, developed over 300 products using peanuts.

12. The first practical telephone was invented by Alexander Graham Bell in 1876.

13. The ballpoint pen was invented by Laszlo Biro in 1938.

14. The first digital camera was created by Kodak engineer Steven Sasson in 1975.

15. Benjamin Franklin invented the lightning rod to protect buildings from lightning strikes.

16. The concept of a "bionic eye" was developed by William Dobelle in the 1970s.

17. The concept of GPS (Global Positioning System) was developed by the U.S. Department of Defense.

18. Charles Goodyear accidentally discovered the process of vulcanization, which led to the creation of rubber.

19. The pacemaker was invented by Wilson Greatbatch in 1958.

20. The Post-it Note was invented by 3M engineer Spencer Silver in 1968.

21. The first practical typewriter was invented by Christopher Latham Sholes in 1868.

22. Johannes Gutenberg invented the printing press around 1440, revolutionizing book production.

23. Hedy Lamarr, an actress, co-invented an early version of frequency hopping, a key technology in wireless communication.

24. The concept of the bar code was developed by Norman Joseph Woodland and Bernard Silver.

25. The first computer virus, named "Creeper," was created in the early 1970s.

26. George de Mestral invented Velcro after being inspired by the burrs that stuck to his dog's fur.

27. The concept of the atomic bomb was developed during the Manhattan Project in the 1940s.

28. The first commercial video game, Pong, was developed by Atari in 1972.

29. The concept of the laser was proposed by Arthur Schawlow and Charles Townes in 1958.

30. The first commercially successful electric car, the GM EV1, was introduced in 1996.

31. The concept of the pacemaker was inspired by an inventor's observation of the rhythmic beating of a heart.

32. The concept of the internet was influenced by ARPANET, a research project funded by the U.S. Department of Defense.

33. The first successful test of a jet engine was conducted by Frank Whittle in 1937.

34. The first successful parachute jump from an airplane was made by André-Jacques Garnerin in 1797.

35. The concept of the airbag was first proposed by John Hetrick in 1953.

36. The concept of the bicycle was developed by Karl Drais in 1817.

37. The concept of the helicopter was inspired by the Chinese toy called the bamboo-copter.

38. The concept of the electric guitar was popularized by Les Paul.

39. The concept of the Frisbee was inspired by the pie tins sold by the Frisbie Pie Company.

40. The concept of the artificial heart was developed by Paul Winchell, the voice of Tigger in Winnie the Pooh.

41. The first successful kidney transplant was performed by Joseph Murray and J. Hartwell Harrison in 1954.

42. The concept of the artificial sweetener saccharin was discovered by Constantine Fahlberg.

43. The concept of the safety razor was developed by King Camp Gillette.

44. The concept of the fire extinguisher was developed by George William Manby in 1818.

45. The concept of the Geiger counter was developed by Hans Geiger and Ernest Rutherford.

46. The concept of the modern condom was developed by Julius Fromm in the early 20th century.

47. The concept of the vacuum cleaner was patented by Hubert Cecil Booth in 1901.

48. The concept of the respirator was developed by John Heysham Gibbon.

49. The concept of the defibrillator was developed by Dr. Paul Zoll in the 1950s.

50. The concept of the cardiac catheterization procedure was developed by Dr. Werner Forssmann.

51. The concept of the insulin pump was developed by Arnold Kadish in the 1960s.

52. The concept of the artificial limb was developed by James Hanger.

53. The concept of the artificial kidney dialysis machine was developed by Willem Kolff.

54. The concept of the first successful liver transplant was developed by Thomas Starzl.

55. The concept of the MRI (magnetic resonance imaging) was developed by Paul Lauterbur and Sir Peter Mansfield.

56. The concept of the electronic ink used in e-readers was developed by Joseph Jacobson.

57. The concept of the first successful heart-lung transplant was developed by Dr. Denton Cooley.

58. The concept of the artificial cornea was developed by Dr. Francis L'Esperance.

59. The concept of the first successful lung transplant was developed by Dr. James Hardy.

60. The concept of the first successful hand transplant was developed by Dr. Jean-Michel Dubernard.

61. The concept of the first successful face transplant was developed by Dr. Jean-Michel Dubernard.

62. The concept of the first successful penis transplant was developed by Dr. André van der Merwe.

63. The concept of the first successful uterus transplant was developed by Dr. Mats Brännström.

64. The concept of the first successful penis and scrotum transplant was developed by Dr. Richard Redett.

65. The concept of the first successful double arm transplant was developed by Dr. L. Scott Levin.

66. The concept of the first successful full face and double hand transplant was developed by Dr. Eduardo Rodríguez.

67. The concept of the first successful simultaneous face and hands transplant was developed by Dr. Laurent Lantieri.

68. The concept of the first successful uterus transplant in the U.S. was developed by Dr. Giuliano Testa.

69. The concept of the first successful pig-to-human heart transplant was developed by Dr. Bartley Griffith.

70. The concept of the first successful pig-to-human kidney transplant was developed by Dr. Joseph Scalea.

# 5

# Technology

1. The first computer mouse was made of wood.

2. Honeywell introduced the first home automation system called "Kitchen Computer" in 1969, but it was too expensive and never became popular.

3. The term "bug" in computer science originated when a moth caused a malfunction in an early computer.

4. The world's first computer programmer was Ada Lovelace, who wrote instructions for Charles Babbage's analytical engine in the mid-1800s.

5. The first mobile phone call was made on April 3, 1973, by Martin Cooper, a Motorola executive.

6. The Apollo 11 mission's computer had less processing power than a modern smartphone.

7. The first 1GB hard drive was introduced in 1980, and it weighed about 550 pounds.

8. The concept of the World Wide Web was proposed by Tim Berners-Lee in 1989.

9. The average person has more computing power in their pocket with a smartphone than NASA had for the moon landing.

10. IBM's Deep Blue became the first computer to defeat a reigning world chess champion, Garry Kasparov, in 1997.

11. The world's first webcam was used to monitor a coffee pot at the University of Cambridge in 1991.

12. The term "Wi-Fi" doesn't stand for anything. It was just a catchy name created by a brand consultancy.

13. The first known computer virus was created in 1983 and was called the Elk Cloner.

14. The world's first 1TB SSD (Solid State Drive) was released in 2008.

15. Amazon started as an online bookstore in 1994 and has since become the largest online retailer globally.

16. The computer mouse was invented by Douglas Engelbart in 1964 and was initially called the "X-Y Position Indicator for a Display System."

17. The first webcam was used to monitor a coffee pot at the University of Cambridge in 1993.

18. The first text message was sent in 1992, and it simply said "Merry Christmas."

19. The first computer virus, named "Brain," was created in 1986.

20. The average smartphone today has more computing power than the computers used for the Apollo 11 moon landing.

21. The first website went live on August 6, 1991.

22. The term "robot" was coined by Czech writer Karel Čapek in his play "R.U.R." in 1920.

23. The first 3D printer was created in 1983 by Chuck Hull.

24. The first computer mouse was made of wood.

25. The first known computer programmer was Ada Lovelace, who wrote instructions for Charles Babbage's analytical engine in the 1840s.

26. The first computer game, "Spacewar!," was created in 1962.

27. The first computer virus, named "Creeper," was created in 1971.

28. The concept of the computer "bit" (binary digit) was introduced by Claude Shannon in 1948.

29. The first computer virus capable of spreading in the wild was the Morris Worm in 1988.

30. The first electronic computer, ENIAC, was completed in 1945 and weighed 30 tons.

31. The world's first 1TB hard drive was released in 2007.

32. The term "cyberspace" was coined by science fiction writer William Gibson in his novel "Neuromancer" in 1984.

33. The first computer with a graphical user interface (GUI) was the Xerox Alto in 1973.

34. The term "bug" in computer science originated when a moth caused a malfunction in an early computer.

35. The first computer password was implemented at MIT in the early 1960s.

36. The first computer mouse was invented by Douglas Engelbart in 1964.

37. The first computer virus, named "Brain," was created in 1986.

38. The first computer virus capable of spreading in the wild was the Morris Worm in 1988.

39. The first computer programmer was Ada Lovelace, who wrote instructions for Charles Babbage's analytical engine in the 1840s.

40. The first computer game, "Spacewar!," was created in 1962.

41. The first computer mouse was made of wood.

42. The first computer virus, named "Creeper," was created in 1971.

43. The first computer with a graphical user interface (GUI) was the Xerox Alto in 1973.

44. The first electronic computer, ENIAC, was completed in 1945 and weighed 30 tons.

45. The first computer virus capable of spreading in the wild was the Morris Worm in 1988.

46. The world's first 1TB hard drive was released in 2007.

47. The first computer password was implemented at MIT in the early 1960s.

48. The term "cyberspace" was coined by science fiction writer William Gibson in his novel "Neuromancer" in 1984.

49. The first computer with a graphical user interface (GUI) was the Xerox Alto in 1973.

50. The term "bug" in computer science originated when a moth caused a malfunction in an early computer.

51. The first computer mouse was made of wood.

52. The first known computer programmer was Ada Lovelace, who wrote instructions for Charles Babbage's analytical engine in the 1840s.

53. The first computer game, "Spacewar!," was created in 1962.

# 6

# Countries

1. Canada has more lakes than the rest of the world combined.

2. The Great Wall of China is not visible from the moon with the naked eye.

3. There are more pyramids in Sudan than in Egypt.

4. Norway introduced salmon sushi to the Japanese in the 80s.

5. Russia is bigger than Pluto.

6. There's a town in Norway called Hell.

7. Australia is wider than the moon.

8. The national anthem of Greece has 158 verses.

9. The world's smallest country, Vatican City, has a population of around 800 people.

10. Turkey spans two continents, Europe and Asia.

11. The Maldives is the lowest country on Earth, with an average ground level of 1.5 meters.

12. Iceland has no mosquitoes.

13. Luxembourg is the only Grand Duchy in the world.

14. Mongolia is the least densely populated country in the world.

15. Madagascar is home to the world's smallest chameleon.

16. The longest place name in the world is in New Zealand: Taumatawhakatangihangakoauauotamateapokaiwhenuakitanatahu.

17. Switzerland has no official capital city.

18. The world's oldest continuously inhabited city is Damascus, Syria.

19. Japan is the country with the most vending machines in the world.

20. Finland has the highest coffee consumption per capita.

21. The United States has the most time zones of any country (11).

22. India is the birthplace of chess.

23. Brazil is named after a tree, not the other way around.

24. Saudi Arabia is the only country in the world without a river.

25. The Philippines is the only Christian-majority country in Asia.

26. Argentina has the world's widest avenue, Avenida 9 de Julio.

27. Egypt is home to the world's oldest known dress.

28. Sweden has the most islands of any country in the world.

29. The longest railway platform is in Gorakhpur, India.

30. Singapore is one of only three surviving city-states in the world.

31. The world's highest navigable lake is Lake Titicaca in Peru.

32. The Great Barrier Reef is the world's largest living structure.

33. Iran is the only country with all 13 climates in the world.

34. Kenya and Ethiopia are the only two countries in Africa that were never colonized.

35. The Amazon rain forest produces 20% of the world's oxygen.

36. South Africa has three capital cities: Pretoria, Cape Town, and Bloemfontein.

37. Bhutan is the only country in the world without traffic lights.

38. The Dead Sea is the lowest point on the Earth's surface.

39. The world's highest waterfall, Angel Falls, is in Venezuela.

40. The highest point in North America is Denali in Alaska.

41. Mongolia is the home of the world's second-largest dinosaur fossil.

42. Greenland has the world's lowest population density.

43. The Panama Canal was one of the largest and most difficult engineering projects ever undertaken.

44. The world's largest desert is Antarctica.

45. Spain is home to the world's second most widely spoken language, Spanish.

46. The oldest university in the world is in Morocco.

47. New Zealand has more sheep than people.

48. The world's tallest tree, Hyperion, is in California.

49. Belgium produces the most chocolate in the world.

50. The longest pleasure beach in the world is in Blackpool, England.

51. The first ever recorded game of baseball was played in Canada.

52. The Netherlands is the world's largest exporter of flowers.

53. The Eiffel Tower can be 15 cm taller during the summer due to thermal expansion.

54. Nigeria has the highest twin birthrate in the world.

55. The world's highest and longest glass bridge is in China.

56. Mount Everest is Earth's highest point above sea level, but not its highest point from base to summit.

57. Mexico City is sinking at a rate of 10 cm per year.

58. The largest sand island in the world is Fraser Island in Australia.

59. Peru has a floating village on Lake Titicaca made entirely of reeds.

60. The Great Barrier Reef is the only living structure visible from space.

61.    Chile is the world's longest country from north to south.

62.    Australia has more than 10,000 beaches.

63.    The world's largest diamond was found in South Africa, weighing 3,106 carats.

64.    Mount Fuji is Japan's highest peak and an active volcano.

65.    The world's largest salt flat, Salar de Uyuni, is in Bolivia.

66.    The Taj Mahal in India was built in memory of the emperor's wife.

67.    Lake Baikal in Russia is the deepest freshwater lake in the world.

68.    Kazakhstan is the world's largest landlocked country.

69.    The Great Wall of Benin in Nigeria is longer than the Great Wall of China.

70.    The first public zoo in the world was opened in Vienna, Austria, in 1752.

# 7

# Language

1.  There are approximately 7,000 languages spoken around the world.

2.  The Basque language, spoken in Spain and France, is not related to any other known language.

3.  The word "alphabet" comes from the first two letters of the Greek alphabet: alpha and beta.

4.  The English word "set" has the highest number of different meanings.

5.  Mandarin Chinese is the most spoken language globally, with over a billion native speakers.

6.  The word "bookkeeper" and "bookkeeping" are the only unhyphenated English words with three consecutive double letters.

7.  The Hawaiian alphabet has only 13 letters.

8.  The longest word in the English language without a vowel is "rhythms."

9.  There are languages, like Pirahã in Brazil, that don't have words for specific numbers.

10. The word "pangram" refers to a sentence that contains every letter of the alphabet at least once.

11. The Russian language has six cases, altering the endings of nouns, pronouns, and adjectives.

12. The word "queue" is the only word in the English language that is still pronounced the same way when the last four letters are removed.

13. "Eunoia" is the shortest word in the English language that contains all five main vowels.

14. The sentence "The quick brown fox jumps over a lazy dog" uses every letter of the alphabet.

15. The Swedish language has a word, "lagom," which roughly translates to "just the right amount."

16. The word "uncopyrightable" is the longest English word that can be written without repeating a letter.

17. The longest word in the English language is
    "pneumonoultramicroscopicsilicovolcanoconiosis," referring to a lung disease
    caused by inhaling very fine silicate or quartz dust.

18. The word "gymnophobia" means the fear of nudity.

19. The second most widely spoken language in the world is Spanish.

20. Inuktitut, spoken in the Arctic regions of Canada, has a variety of words for snow,
    reflecting the importance of the concept in their culture.

21. The word "hello" wasn't commonly used as a greeting until the invention of the
    telephone.

22. The Welsh language has the longest place name in Europe:
    Llanfairpwllgwyngyllgogerychwyrndrobwllllantysiliogogogoch.

23. The sentence "Buffalo buffalo Buffalo buffalo buffalo buffalo Buffalo buffalo" is
    grammatically correct.

24. The word "nerd" was first coined by Dr. Seuss in "If I Ran the Zoo" in 1950.

25. The term "OK" originated during the 1830s fad of intentionally misspelling
    words.

26. The sentence "I am" is the shortest complete sentence in the English language.

27. The Basque language is considered a language isolate, with no known linguistic
    relatives.

28. There are more English words beginning with the letter 'S' than any other letter.

29. The word "alphabet" is derived from the first two Greek letters, alpha and beta.

30. The word "typewriter" is the longest word that can be typed using only one row
    of a QWERTY keyboard.

31. The word "hippopotomonstrosesquippedaliophobia" means the fear of long
    words.

32. Sign languages, like American Sign Language (ASL), are complete and complex
    languages with their own grammar and syntax.

33. The first English dictionary was created by Samuel Johnson in 1755.

34. The word "karaoke" means "empty orchestra" in Japanese.

35. The sentence "James, while John had had "had," had had "had had"; "had had"
    had had a better effect on the teacher" is grammatically correct.

36. The word "nerd" was first coined by Dr. Seuss in "If I Ran the Zoo" in 1950.

37. The Hawaiian language has only 13 letters.

38. The sentence "The quick brown fox jumps over a lazy dog" uses every letter of
    the alphabet.

39. The term "dord" appeared in the Webster's New International Dictionary from
    1934 to 1939 as a synonym for density.

40. The sentence "The quick brown fox jumps over a lazy dog" uses every letter of the alphabet.

41. The longest word without a vowel is "rhythms."

42. The word "palindrome" is a palindrome; it reads the same backward as forward.

43. The sentence "The quick brown fox jumps over a lazy dog" uses every letter of the alphabet.

44. The longest word without a vowel is "rhythms."

45. The word "bookkeeper" and "bookkeeping" are the only unhyphenated English words with three consecutive double letters.

46. The Basque language, spoken in Spain and France, is not related to any other known language.

47. The sentence "Buffalo buffalo Buffalo buffalo buffalo buffalo Buffalo buffalo" is grammatically correct.

48. The word "uncopyrightable" is the longest English word that can be written without repeating a letter.

49. The sentence "Buffalo buffalo Buffalo buffalo buffalo buffalo Buffalo buffalo" is grammatically correct.

50. The longest word without a vowel is "rhythms."

51. The word "gymnophobia" means the fear of nudity.

52. The term "dord" appeared in the Webster's New International Dictionary from 1934 to 1939 as a synonym for density.

53. The sentence "I am" is the shortest complete sentence in the English language.

54. The sentence "James, while John had had "had," had had "had had"; "had had" had had a better effect on the teacher" is grammatically correct.

55. The word "bookkeeper" and "bookkeeping" are the only unhyphenated English words with three consecutive double letters.

56. The Basque language is considered a language isolate, with no known linguistic relatives.

57. The term "OK" originated during the 1830s fad of intentionally misspelling words.

58. The word "typewriter" is the longest word that can be typed using only one row of a QWERTY keyboard.

59. The sentence "James, while John had had "had," had had "had had"; "had had" had had a better effect on the teacher" is grammatically correct.

60. The word "karaoke" means "empty orchestra" in Japanese.

61. The Hawaiian alphabet has only 13 letters.

62. The sentence "I am" is the shortest complete sentence in the English language.

63. The word "nerd" was first coined by Dr. Seuss in "If I Ran the Zoo" in 1950.

64. The word "uncopyrightable" is the longest English word that can be written without repeating a letter.

65. Sign languages, like American Sign Language (ASL), are complete and complex languages with their own grammar and syntax.

66. The word "alphabet" is derived from the first two Greek letters, alpha and beta.

67. The longest word in the English language is "pneumonoultramicroscopicsilicovolcanoconiosis," referring to a lung disease caused by inhaling very fine silicate or quartz dust.

68. The word "queue" is the only word in the English language that is still pronounced the same way when the last four letters are removed.

69. The sentence "Buffalo buffalo Buffalo buffalo buffalo buffalo Buffalo buffalo" is grammatically correct.

70. The Swedish language has a word, "lagom," which roughly translates to "just the right amount."

# 8

# Movie

1. The longest film ever made is "Logistics," with a runtime of 51 days.
2. The word "mafia" is never mentioned in the film "The Godfather."
3. The first motion picture was only about 4 seconds long.
4. The "Matrix" trilogy's code is just recipes from a sushi cookbook.
5. The Wilhelm Scream is a stock sound effect used in over 400 movies.
6. The first movie with a feature-length computer-generated character was "Young Sherlock Holmes" in 1985.
7. The highest-grossing R-rated movie is "Joker."
8. "Gone with the Wind" is the highest-grossing film of all time when adjusted for inflation.
9. The first film to use the term "OMG" was "1917."
10. The famous shower scene in "Psycho" took seven days to shoot.
11. The average person blinks 28,800 times per day, and a 2-hour movie has around 172,800 frames.
12. "Clerks" was shot for only $27,575 in the convenience store where director Kevin Smith worked.
13. The word "smurf" is used 247 times in the movie "The Smurfs."
14. The longest-running film in cinema history is "The Rocky Horror Picture Show."
15. The actors in "127 Hours" had to wear the same clothes for the entire filming process.
16. "Avatar" was the first film to gross over $2 billion.
17. The phrase "Beam me up, Scotty" was never said in the original Star Trek series.
18. The language spoken by the Minions in "Despicable Me" is a combination of French, Spanish, English, and gibberish.
19. "Pulp Fiction" contains more than 265 uses of the F-word.
20. The "Star Wars" opening crawl was inspired by Flash Gordon.
21. The Wachowskis had four weeks of intense martial arts training before filming "The Matrix."
22. The first feature film ever made was "The Story of the Kelly Gang" in 1906.
23. "E.T. the Extra-Terrestrial" was originally a horror film titled "Night Skies."

24. The "Back to the Future" DeLorean was supposed to be a refrigerator.

25. The longest fight scene in cinema history is 51 minutes long and takes place in "They Live."

26. The first film to use the term "OMG" was "1917."

27. "Die Hard" is based on a novel called "Nothing Lasts Forever."

28. The "Jurassic Park" dinosaur sounds were made from recordings of tortoise mating rituals.

29. "Titanic" was the first film to make over a billion dollars.

30. The "Terminator" budget was so tight that Arnold Schwarzenegger didn't receive a salary.

31. "Casablanca" is widely considered one of the greatest films ever, yet it was rushed and made on a tight schedule.

32. The "James Bond" series is the most successful film franchise in history.

33. The "Halloween" theme was composed in just a few days.

34. The longest continuous shot in film history is in "Russian Ark."

35. Stanley Kubrick's "The Shining" has a hedge maze that never existed.

36. The iconic "I feel the need—the need for speed" line from "Top Gun" was ad-libbed.

37. The sound of the velociraptors in "Jurassic Park" is a recording of mating tortoises.

38. "Forrest Gump" author Winston Groom never expected the film to be made.

39. The "Star Wars" lightsaber sound is a combination of the hum of an old television and the buzz from a film projector motor.

40. Alfred Hitchcock's "Rope" was filmed with only 10 long takes.

41. "The Dark Knight" had a 4-hour cut that was later edited down.

42. The "Lord of the Rings" trilogy was shot in 274 days, back-to-back.

43. The first film to feature a flushing toilet was "Psycho."

44. "The Blair Witch Project" was made on a budget of $22,000 but grossed over $240 million.

45. Marilyn Monroe was the first-ever Playmate in Playboy magazine in 1953.

46. The original title for "The Matrix" was "The Third Eye."

47. "The Wizard of Oz" was one of the first movies to be in color.

48. The "Harry Potter" films were the highest-grossing film series until surpassed by the Marvel Cinematic Universe.

49. The blood used in "Psycho" was actually chocolate syrup.

50. The longest-running movie in theaters is "The Rocky Horror Picture Show."

51. The "Jurassic Park" T. rex roar is a mix of a baby elephant, a tiger, and an alligator.

52. Steven Spielberg directed "Jurassic Park" while also working on "Schindler's List."

53. The "Indiana Jones" character was named after George Lucas's dog.

54. The "Fast and Furious" franchise was inspired by a magazine article about street racing.

55. The first film to use CGI was "Westworld" in 1973.

56. The "Planet of the Apes" makeup took up to 3.5 hours to apply.

57. The "Ewok" language in "Return of the Jedi" is a combination of Tibetan and Nepalese.

58. "Jaws" had a mechanical shark named Bruce.

59. "The Simpsons Movie" took 18 years to make.

60. The "Hobbit" trilogy has a longer combined runtime than "The Lord of the Rings" trilogy.

61. "The Exorcist" was the first horror film to be nominated for a Best Picture Oscar.

62. The first film ever made in Hollywood was "In Old California" in 1910.

63. The "Mad Max" series was almost entirely dubbed in post-production.

64. "The Silence of the Lambs" is the only horror film to win the Best Picture Oscar.

65. The "Star Wars" opening crawl was created using practical effects.

66. The "Mission: Impossible" theme was written in just three minutes.

67. "The Lord of the Rings: The Return of the King" won all 11 Oscars it was nominated for.

68. The "Terminator" was originally envisioned as a cyborg killing machine with a different actor playing the human version.

69. The word "robot" was introduced to the world in the play "R.U.R." (Rossum's Universal Robots) in 1920.

70. The first feature-length animated film is "Snow White and the Seven Dwarfs."

# 9

# Pop

1. The term "pop" is short for "popular music," encompassing a wide range of genres.
2. The first recorded use of the term "pop music" dates back to 1926.
3. Michael Jackson's "Thriller" is the best-selling pop album of all time.
4. The Beatles hold the record for the most No. 1 hits on the Billboard Hot 100.
5. The world's first pop chart was published in the United States in 1940.
6. The most expensive music video ever made is Michael and Janet Jackson's "Scream."
7. ABBA's "Dancing Queen" was the first pop song to be performed at the White House.
8. The synthesizer revolutionized pop music in the 1980s.
9. "Gangnam Style" by Psy became the first YouTube video to reach one billion views.
10. The "Pop Goes the Weasel" nursery rhyme dates back to the 1700s.
11. The pop icon Madonna has sold over 300 million records worldwide.
12. "Bohemian Rhapsody" by Queen is one of the longest pop songs to top the charts.
13. The term "bubblegum pop" refers to catchy, upbeat pop music.
14. The Spice Girls' "Wannabe" was the first single by a girl group to reach No. 1 in 17 countries.
15. The pop genre has roots in various musical styles, including jazz, blues, and folk.
16. The word "pop" can also refer to the sound made by bubbles bursting.
17. Elvis Presley's hip-shaking moves were considered controversial in the 1950s.
18. The first music video ever aired on MTV was "Video Killed the Radio Star" by The Buggles.
19. The pop singer Prince was known for his mastery of multiple instruments.
20. "Like a Virgin" by Madonna was her first No. 1 single on the Billboard Hot 100.
21. The Jackson 5's "I Want You Back" was their first hit single.
22. The term "boy band" was first used in the late 1980s.
23. Britney Spears' "…Baby One More Time" is one of the best-selling singles of all time.

24. The Bee Gees' "Stayin' Alive" is often associated with the disco era.

25. Pop music often reflects and influences fashion trends.

26. The first Grammy Awards were held in 1959, and Domenico Modugno's "Nel Blu Dipinto Di Blu (Volare)" won Record of the Year.

27. "I Will Always Love You" by Whitney Houston is one of the best-selling singles by a female artist.

28. The Backstreet Boys' "I Want It That Way" is considered a classic boy band anthem.

29. The first concert held at the Sydney Opera House featured pop superstar Paul Robeson.

30. Adele's "Rolling in the Deep" is one of the best-selling digital singles.

31. The pop genre has inspired numerous dance crazes, from the Twist to the Harlem Shake.

32. The term "crossover hit" refers to a song that achieves success in multiple genres.

33. Lady Gaga's real name is Stefani Joanne Angelina Germanotta.

34. The Beatles' "Hey Jude" was originally titled "Hey Jules."

35. The term "teenybopper" was coined in the 1960s to describe young fans of pop music.

36. Whitney Houston's version of "I Will Always Love You" spent 14 weeks at No. 1 on the Billboard Hot 100.

37. The pop band ABBA is an acronym of the members' names: Agnetha, Björn, Benny, and Anni-Frid.

38. "Wake Me Up Before You Go-Go" by Wham! was inspired by a note Andrew Ridgeley left for his parents.

39. The term "One-Hit Wonder" describes an artist known for only one popular song.

40. The pop group *NSYNC was formed by Lou Pearlman, who later went to prison for fraud.

41. Madonna's birth name is Madonna Louise Ciccone.

42. The world's first pop star was considered to be Franz Liszt in the 19th century.

43. "Baby Got Back" by Sir Mix-a-Lot is known for its humorous lyrics about curvy women.

44. The Pet Shop Boys took their name from friends who worked in a pet shop.

45. "Uptown Funk" by Mark Ronson featuring Bruno Mars spent 14 consecutive weeks at No. 1.

46. The first pop song to be released on a 45 RPM record was "Pee Wee King & His Golden West Cowboys."

47. The term "pop art" describes an art movement that emerged in the 1950s.

48. "Despacito" by Luis Fonsi and Daddy Yankee became the most-watched YouTube video of all time.

49. The term "blue-eyed soul" refers to white artists who sing in a soulful, R&B style.

50. "Smooth" by Santana featuring Rob Thomas holds the record for the longest-running No. 1 song on the Billboard Hot 100.

51. The Spice Girls' nicknames were Sporty, Baby, Scary, Posh, and Ginger.

52. The term "Mashup" refers to a song created by blending elements from two or more tracks.

53. Michael Jackson's "Billie Jean" was the first video by a black artist to be played in heavy rotation on MTV.

54. The pop genre often incorporates elements of electronic music.

55. The term "girl power" was popularized by the Spice Girls.

56. The first pop song to use auto-tune was Cher's "Believe."

57. "All About That Bass" by Meghan Trainor promotes body positivity.

58. The Beatles' final live performance was on the rooftop of Apple Corps in London.

59. The term "rock and roll" was initially used as a euphemism for sex.

60. Katy Perry's "Roar" was inspired by the boxing film "Rocky."

61. The pop genre has been influenced by Latin music, evident in hits like "Livin' la Vida Loca" by Ricky Martin.

62. "Happy" by Pharrell Williams became a global anthem of positivity.

63. The term "sampling" involves using a portion of a sound recording in another song.

64. "YMCA" by the Village People became an anthem for the LGBTQ+ community.

65. The pop icon Elton John has over 4,000 pairs of glasses.

66. The term "fanzine" originated in the pop music scene to describe fan-created magazines.

67. "Rolling Stone" magazine's first issue featured a photo of John Lennon.

68. The pop group TLC stands for Tionne, Lisa, and Crystal (a former member).

69. The first pop music awards were the Gramophone Awards, initiated in 1959.

70. "Sugar, Sugar" by The Archies is the only fictional band to have a No. 1 hit on the Billboard Hot 100.

# 10

# History and culture

1. The Great Wall of China is visible from space, but so is the Amazon Rainforest, which is often underestimated.

2. Cleopatra, the last pharaoh of Egypt, lived closer in time to the moon landing than the construction of the Great Pyramid of Giza.

3. The ancient Egyptians worshipped a sky goddess named Nut, who was believed to swallow the sun each night and give birth to it every morning.

4. The concept of zero in mathematics was developed by the ancient Maya civilization.

5. The city of Rome was founded in 753 BCE, and it's older than the country of Germany, which was established in 1871.

6. The Eiffel Tower in Paris can be 15 cm taller during the summer due to the expansion of iron in the heat.

7. The oldest known recipe is for beer and dates back to around 6,000 BCE in ancient Sumeria.

8. The city of Istanbul was previously known as Byzantium and later as Constantinople before being renamed in 1930.

9. The hanging gardens of Babylon, one of the Seven Wonders of the Ancient World, might not have existed; some historians argue that it's a myth.

10. The Great Fire of London in 1666 reportedly started in a bakery on Pudding Lane and lasted for three days, destroying much of the city.

11. The shortest war in history was between Britain and Zanzibar in 1896, lasting only 38 minutes.

12. The first recorded joke dates back to ancient Sumeria around 1900 BCE.

13. The word "nerd" was first coined by Dr. Seuss in "If I Ran the Zoo" in 1950.

14. The Colosseum in Rome could be filled with water to stage naval battles for public entertainment.

15. The world's oldest known system of writing is cuneiform, developed by the Sumerians around 3200 BCE.

16. The word "sincere" comes from the Latin words "sine" (without) and "cera" (wax) because Romans used to fill in cracks in statues with wax.

17. The city of Venice is built on a network of 118 islands connected by over 400 bridges.

18. The Mayans used rubber balls for sports, and the winner was often sacrificed to the gods.

19. The ancient Greeks had a festival called "Krypteia" where young men were encouraged to sneak around and assassinate helot slaves.

20. The Great Pyramid of Giza originally had a smooth, white limestone casing that reflected the sun's light, making it shine like a "gem" in the desert.

21. The concept of the weekend as we know it today was not widely adopted until the early 20th century.

22. The first recorded Olympic Games took place in 776 BCE in Olympia, Greece.

23. The tradition of exchanging wedding rings dates back to ancient Egypt, where rings were seen as symbols of eternity.

24. The Gutenberg Bible, printed in 1455, was the first major book printed using movable type in the West.

25. The ancient city of Mohenjo-Daro, part of the Indus Valley Civilization, had advanced urban planning with a sophisticated sewage system.

26. The Trojan War, famously depicted in Homer's "Iliad," may have been based on historical events, but the details remain uncertain.

27. The first recorded music concert was held in 1739 at the Foundling Hospital in London.

28. The longest-reigning monarch in British history is Queen Elizabeth II, who ascended to the throne in 1952.

29. The concept of democracy originated in ancient Greece, particularly in the city-state of Athens.

30. The Silk Road was a network of trade routes that connected the East and West, facilitating cultural exchange and commerce.

31. The Aztecs used cocoa beans as a form of currency, and chocolate was consumed as a bitter beverage in their culture.

32. The Black Death, one of the deadliest pandemics in human history, is estimated to have killed 75–200 million people in the 14th century.

33. The concept of the compass in navigation was introduced to Europe by the Chinese explorer Zheng He in the 15th century.

34. The first recorded use of the term "genius" was in ancient Rome, where it referred to a guardian spirit or deity.

35. The Library of Alexandria, one of the largest and most significant libraries of the ancient world, was destroyed in multiple incidents, and its exact location remains unknown.

36. The Great Famine in Ireland from 1845 to 1852 led to the deaths of approximately one million people and mass emigration.

37. The tradition of carving pumpkins for Halloween originated from the Irish practice of carving turnips.

38. The Great Depression, a severe worldwide economic downturn, began in 1929 and lasted throughout the 1930s.

39. The concept of time zones was first proposed by Sir Sandford Fleming at the International Meridian Conference in 1884.

40. The city of Petra in Jordan, famous for its rock-cut architecture, was a thriving trade hub in ancient times.

41. The Gutenberg press revolutionized printing and played a crucial role in the spread of the Renaissance and Reformation.

42. The tradition of shaking hands as a greeting dates back to ancient Greece, symbolizing that both parties were not carrying weapons.

43. The construction of the pyramids at Giza required an immense workforce, but evidence suggests that the laborers were skilled and well-fed, dispelling the notion of slaves building the pyramids.

44. The concept of human rights has ancient roots, with documents like the Magna Carta (1215) and the Bill of Rights (1689) contributing to its development.

45. The ancient city of Rome had public toilets known as "cloacinae," and people used a sponge on a stick for personal hygiene.

46. The concept of the Mona Lisa's smile being elusive is due to the phenomenon of "uncertain smiles," where the expression appears to change depending on your viewing angle.

47. The Rosetta Stone, discovered in 1799, played a crucial role in deciphering ancient Egyptian hieroglyphs.

48. The hanging coffins of Sagada in the Philippines are suspended on cliffs, a unique burial tradition believed to bring the deceased closer to ancestral spirits.

49. The Taj Mahal in India was built by Emperor Shah Jahan in memory of his wife Mumtaz Mahal and took around 22 years to complete.

50. The concept of the internet was proposed by J.C.R. Licklider in the 1960s, envisioning a "Galactic Network" that would allow users to access data and programs from any site.

51. The city of Istanbul was formerly known as Byzantium and later as Constantinople before being renamed in 1930.

52. The concept of the Turing Test, a measure of a machine's ability to exhibit intelligent behavior indistinguishable from that of a human, was introduced by Alan Turing in 1950.

53. The ancient city of Pompeii was preserved by the volcanic ash of Mount Vesuvius in 79 CE, providing a unique snapshot of Roman daily life.

54. The concept of the Fibonacci sequence, where each number is the sum of the two preceding ones, was introduced to the West by Leonardo of Pisa in his book "Liber Abaci."

55. The city of Timbuktu in Mali was a center of learning and trade in the medieval era, attracting scholars and merchants from across Africa and the Middle East.

56. The tradition of the Olympic flame being lit at Olympia and carried to the host city began in the 1936 Berlin Olympics.

57. The Great Zimbabwe, a medieval city in southeastern Africa, was an important center of trade and culture.

58. The concept of the metric system was first proposed during the French Revolution in the late 18th century.

59. The concept of "guerrilla warfare" originated during the Peninsular War (1808–1814) when Spanish irregulars used hit-and-run tactics against French forces.

60. The Terracotta Army in China, discovered in 1974, consists of thousands of life-sized clay soldiers buried with Emperor Qin Shi Huang to accompany him in the afterlife.

61. The concept of the placebo effect, where patients experience improvements due to the belief that they are receiving treatment, has been observed since ancient times.

62. The ancient city of Carthage was a major power in the Mediterranean until its destruction by the Romans in the Third Punic War.

63. The concept of the "butterfly effect," where small changes can have far-reaching consequences, is a principle of chaos theory introduced by Edward Lorenz.

64. The city of Troy, depicted in Homer's "Iliad," was thought to be mythical until its discovery by archaeologist Heinrich Schliemann in the late 19th century.

65. The concept of the Higgs boson, a fundamental particle, was proposed in the 1960s and confirmed by experiments at CERN in 2012.

66. The ancient city of Machu Picchu in Peru was built by the Inca emperor Pachacuti in the 15th century and abandoned during the Spanish Conquest.

67. The concept of the Scientific Revolution in the 16th and 17th centuries challenged traditional views and laid the foundation for modern science.

68. The Great Barrier Reef, the world's largest coral reef system, is composed of over 2,900 individual reefs and 900 islands.

69. The concept of the "Big Bang," the prevailing cosmological model explaining the origin of the universe, was proposed in the 20th century.

70. The ancient Greeks believed in a place called Hyperborea, a mythical land beyond the North Wind where people lived in eternal happiness.

# 11

## Creation

1. The universe is estimated to be around 13.8 billion years old.
2. Every atom in your body is billions of years old, as they were created in stars that exploded.
3. Earth formed about 4.54 billion years ago.
4. The first life on Earth likely appeared around 3.5 billion years ago.
5. The human brain is the most energy-consuming organ in the body, using about 20% of the body's total energy.
6. In a single day, a human heart can pump enough blood to fill a small swimming pool.
7. Humans share about 50% of their DNA with bananas.
8. The oldest known living organism is a colony of sea grass in the Mediterranean, estimated to be about 200,000 years old.
9. The human body has more bacterial cells than human cells.
10. Octopuses have three hearts and blue blood.
11. The deepest part of the ocean, the Challenger Deep, reaches a depth of about 36,070 feet (10,994 meters).
12. The Great Wall of China is visible from space, but only under certain conditions.
13. Honey never spoils. Archaeologists have found pots of honey in ancient Egyptian tombs that are over 3,000 years old and still perfectly edible.
14. The first recorded recipe dates back to around 4000 BC and is for beer.
15. There are more possible iterations of a game of chess than there are atoms in the observable universe.
16. The Eiffel Tower can be 15 cm taller during the summer due to thermal expansion.
17. A day on Venus (one full rotation) is longer than a year on Venus (one full orbit around the sun).
18. The largest desert in the world is Antarctica.
19. Humans and giraffes have the same number of neck vertebrae (seven).
20. A single rain forest can produce 20% of the world's oxygen.

21. The oldest known living tree is a Great Basin bristle cone pine named Methuselah, over 4,800 years old.
22. The largest volcano in our solar system is on Mars and is called Olympus Mons.
23. Cows have best friends and can become stressed when they are separated.
24. There is a species of jellyfish known as Turritopsis dohrnii that is considered biologically immortal.
25. The color of a carrot used to be purple, not orange.
26. The total weight of all the ants on Earth is comparable to that of all the humans on Earth.
27. Honeybees can recognize human faces.
28. The Northern Hemisphere has more landmass than the Southern Hemisphere.
29. The Earth's core is as hot as the surface of the sun.
30. The probability of you drinking a glass of water that contains a molecule of water that also passed through a dinosaur is high.
31. Cows have a magnetic sense and tend to align themselves with the Earth's magnetic field.
32. There are more stars in the universe than there are grains of sand on all the beaches on Earth.
33. The speed of light is about 186,282 miles per second (299,792 kilometers per second).
34. The Andromeda Galaxy is on a collision course with the Milky Way and will collide in about 4 billion years.
35. The smell of freshly cut grass is actually a plant distress call.
36. The shortest war in history was between Britain and Zanzibar in 1896, lasting only 38 minutes.
37. The longest continuous human civilization is in China, with a history dating back over 4,000 years.
38. The Great Barrier Reef is the largest living structure on Earth and can be seen from space.
39. Bananas are berries, but strawberries aren't.
40. The number of possible ways to shuffle a deck of cards is so large that every time you shuffle a deck, it's likely the first time in history that exact order has existed.
41. A day on Mars is about 24.6 hours.
42. The longest time a person has survived without sleep is 11 days.
43. The world's largest desert was not always a desert; the Sahara used to be a lush and green region.
44. The Earth's atmosphere weighs around 5.5 quadrillion tons.

45. Humans and giraffes have the same number of neck vertebrae (seven).

46. The smallest bone in the human body is the stapes bone in the ear.

47. The longest word without a vowel is "rhythms."

48. The fingerprints of koala bears are virtually indistinguishable from those of humans.

49. Honey never spoils. Archaeologists have found pots of honey in ancient Egyptian tombs that are over 3,000 years old and still perfectly edible.

50. The moon is moving away from Earth at a rate of about 1.5 inches (3.8 centimeters) per year.

51. The Great Wall of China is not visible from the moon with the naked eye.

52. An average person will spend six months of their life waiting for red lights to turn green.

53. A "jiffy" is an actual unit of time, equivalent to 1/100th of a second.

54. The world's largest volcano is not on Earth but on Mars. Olympus Mons is about 13.6 miles (22 kilometers) high, almost three times the height of Mount Everest.

55. A teaspoonful of neutron star material would weigh about 6 billion tons.

56. The human brain generates about 20 watts of electrical power while awake.

57. Jupiter's moon Europa has an ocean beneath its icy surface that contains more than twice the amount of water found on Earth.

58. The Sahara Desert can reach temperatures of up to 136 degrees Fahrenheit (57.7 degrees Celsius).

59. The Great Pyramid of Giza originally stood at 146.6 meters (481 feet), but erosion and the loss of the outer casing stones have reduced its height to 138.8 meters (455 feet).

60. The Earth's rotation is gradually slowing, at a rate of approximately 17 milliseconds per hundred years.

61. The speed of Earth's orbit around the Sun is about 67,000 miles per hour (107,000 kilometers per hour).

62. The driest desert on Earth is the Atacama Desert in South America.

63. The largest canyon in the solar system is Valles Marineris on Mars, reaching depths of up to 7 kilometers (23,000 feet).

64. The world's largest ocean, the Pacific Ocean, covers an area larger than all the Earth's landmass combined.

65. The oldest known impact crater on Earth is the Vredefort Crater in South Africa, estimated to be about 2 billion years old.

66. A day on Pluto is about 6.4 Earth days long.

67. The longest mountain range on Earth is the Mid-Atlantic Ridge, extending for about 16,000 kilometers (10,000 miles).

68. The highest recorded temperature on Earth is 134 degrees Fahrenheit (56.7 degrees Celsius) in Furnace Creek Ranch, Death Valley, California.

69. The coldest temperature ever recorded on Earth is -128.6 degrees Fahrenheit (-89.2 degrees Celsius) in Antarctica.

70. The International Space Station (ISS) travels at a speed of about 28,000 kilometers per hour (17,500 miles per hour) and completes an orbit around Earth approximately every 90 minutes.